C.1

Many Ways to Move
A Look at Motion

Jennifer Boothroyd

Lerner Publications Company
Minneapolis

To Alyssa, Olivia, Hannah, and Monica

Lerner Publications Company
A division of Lerner Publishing Group, Inc.
241 First Avenue North
Minneapolis, MN 55401 U.S.A.

Website address: www.lernerbooks.com

Library of Congress Cataloging-in-Publication Data

Boothroyd, Jennifer, 1972-
    Many Ways to Move: A Look at Motion / by Jennifer Boothroyd.
        p.   cm. — (Lightning bolt books™—Exploring Physical Science)
    Includes index.
    ISBN 978-0-7613-5434-5 (lib. bdg. : alk. paper)
    1. Motion—Juvenile literature. 2. Force and energy—Juvenile literature. I. Title.
    QC127.4.B66 2011
    531.11—dc22   2009037702

Manufactured in the United States of America
1 — BP — 7/15/10

Contents

Lots of Motion

Things are in motion everywhere. Zooooom! An airplane soars through the sky.

Whooosshhh!

A wind gust blows
through the leaves.

Vrrroom! A motorcycle races down the track.

Forces Make Motion

Objects are in motion when they move from one place to another. A force puts an object in motion. A force is a push or a pull.

A force put this swing in motion.

When you push a door, it moves away from you.

When you pull a door, it
moves closer to you.

Gravity pulls on this tree's leaves. They float to the ground.

Gravity is a force that pulls leaves and other objects down to Earth's surface.

The wind blows. It pushes this kite higher in the air.

The force of the wind pushes this boy's kite toward the clouds.

Ways Things Move

Things move in different ways.

A gymnast walks in a straight line.

A skier zigzags down a hill.

A dreidel spins.

A Ferris wheel moves in a circular motion.

A child bounces
up
and
down.

A tail wags
back and forth.

Some objects move back and forth or up and down very quickly. **This fast motion is called a vibration.** Guitar strings vibrate.

Plucking a guitar's strings makes the strings vibrate. The strings make a sound when they vibrate.

How Much Motion?

Motion can be measured by how far something moved. This girl climbed 6 feet (1.8 meters) up the wall.

This car drove for miles.

This bug crawled 2 inches (5 centimeters).

Motion can also be measured by speed. Speed is how quickly or slowly something moves.

Race cars move at a very high speed.

A weak force makes something move slowly. Your breath makes a toy boat move slowly.

A strong force makes something move quickly. The wind makes a sailboat travel quickly.

Changing Motion

A force can change
an object's direction.

A soccer
player kicks
the ball toward
the goal.

The goalie
kicks the
ball away.

Forces can also change an object's speed. Friction is a force. It slows things down or makes them stop. Friction is caused when two objects rub together.

Friction makes this car move slowly on the carpet. The car's tires rubbing on the carpet creates friction.

Air resistance is friction caused when an object moves in the air. Air resistance slows down motion. It helps this skydiver float down to the ground.

Air rubbing against the skydiver's parachute slows the skydiver down.

Bicycle racers wear special clothing to make less air resistance. They want to go faster.

This racer's smooth suit and helmet make little air resistance.

Changing directions can change an object's speed. A car driving down a zigzag street goes slower than one driving in a straight line.

This street in Burlington, Iowa, is called Snake Alley. People must drive very slowly on this street. It's hard to make a car drive in a zigzag if it's moving fast.

Our planet and the people on it are constantly in motion. What are some of the ways you move?

Activity
Air Soccer

Most people make a soccer ball move with their feet (and sometimes their hands). Can you play soccer without touching the ball? In this game, you will use your breath to make the ball move across the field.

What you need:

tape

2 foam or plastic fruit baskets

a small box lid

a Ping-Pong ball

a friend

two straws

What you do:

1. Tape the baskets on their sides at each end of the box lid. The lid is the field, and the boxes are the goals.

2. Place the ball in the center of the field.

3. Sit on one side of the field, and have your friend sit at the other side.

4. Take a straw, and give the other one to your friend. Use the straws to try to blow the ball into each other's goal.

5. Once the ball goes into someone's goal, put it back in the middle, and play again.

Glossary

air resistance: friction caused when an object moves in the air

direction: the way that someone or something is moving

force: a push or a pull

friction: a force that slows things down or makes them stop. Rubbing creates friction.

gravity: a force that pulls things down toward the surface of Earth

motion: movement

speed: the rate at which something moves

vibration: a fast back-and-forth or up-and-down motion

Further Reading

Dragonfly TV: Curling
http://pbskids.org/dragonflytv/show/curling.html

Mason, Adrienne. *Move It!: Motion, Forces, and You.* Toronto: Kids Can Press, 2005.

Nelson, Robin. *Ways Things Move.* Minneapolis: Lerner Publications Company, 2004.

Physics4Kids: Motion
http://www.physics4kids.com/files/motion_intro.html

Science of Baseball: Thrown for a Curve
http://www.exploratorium.edu/baseball/curve.html

Stewart, Melissa. *Energy in Motion.* New York: Children's Press, 2006.

Index

Photo Acknowledgments

The images in this book are used with the permission of: © Stock Connection Blue/ Alamy, p. 2; © iStockphoto.com/Simon Alvinge, p. 4; © Cultura Limited/SuperStock, p. 5; © Emportes JM/Stock Image/Getty Images, p. 6; © Stockbyte/Getty Images, p. 7; © PhotoAlto Agency RF/Getty Images, p. 8; © Birgid Allig/Cusp/Photolibrary, p. 9; © Raymond Forbes/SuperStock/Photolibrary, p. 10; © RT images/Shutterstock Images, p. 11; © Picture Partners/Alamy, p. 12 (left); © Koji Aoki/AFLO Royalty Free/Photolibrary, p. 12 (right); © Michele Westmorland/Photodisc/Getty Images, p. 13 (top); © iStockphoto.com/ArtmannWitte, p. 13 (bottom); © Barbara Peacock/Taxi/Getty Images, p. 14 (top); © Deborah Bardowicks/Oxford Scientific/Photolibrary, p. 14 (bottom); © iStockphoto.com/Vladimir Bikhovskly, p. 15; © David Woodfall/ Photographers Choice/Getty Images, p. 16; Blend Images/PBNJ Productions /Getty Images, p. 17; © iStockphoto.com/mammamaart, p. 18; © Colin Anderson/ Photographer's Choice/Getty Images, p. 19; © Photononstop/SuperStock, p. 20; © Terje Rakke/Stone/Getty Images, p. 21; © Ableimages/Riser/Getty Images, p. 22 (top left); © Jack Sullivan/Alamy, p. 22 (right); © Bader-Butowski/Westend61/Photolibrary, p. 23; © Brendon Thorne/Getty Images, p. 24; © Friedmann Vogel/Bongarts/Getty Images, p. 25; AP Photo/The Hawk Eye, Melissa Jansson, p. 26; © iStockphoto.com/Lawrence Sawyer, p. 27; © Todd Strand/Independent Picture Service, pp. 28–29; © Oliver Furrer/ Brand X Pictures/Getty Images, p. 30; © iStockphoto.com/Tammy Bryngelson, p. 31.

Front cover: © Mark D. Maziarz/age fotostock/Photolibrary, (snowboard); © Erik Isakson/Getty Images, (pogo stock); © manfredxy/Shutterstock Images (ferris wheel).